HOW CAN I
HONOR CHRIST IN FIGHTING CANCER?

✘ Cultivating Biblical Godliness

Series Editors
Joel R. Beeke and Ryan M. McGraw

Dr. D. Martyn Lloyd-Jones once said that what the church needs to do most of all is "to begin herself to live the Christian life. If she did that, men and women would be crowding into our buildings. They would say, 'What is the secret of this?'" As Christians, one of our greatest needs is for the Spirit of God to cultivate biblical godliness in us in order to put the beauty of Christ on display through us, all to the glory of the triune God. With this goal in mind, this series of booklets treats matters vital to Christian experience at a basic level. Each booklet addresses a specific question in order to inform the mind, warm the affections, and transform the whole person by the Spirit's grace, so that the church may adorn the doctrine of God our Savior in all things.

HOW CAN I
HONOR CHRIST IN FIGHTING CANCER?

EARL M. BLACKBURN

REFORMATION HERITAGE BOOKS
GRAND RAPIDS, MICHIGAN

How Can I Honor Christ in Fighting Cancer?
© 2017 by Earl M. Blackburn

All rights reserved. No part of this book may be used or reproduced in any manner whatsoever without written permission except in the case of brief quotations embodied in critical articles and reviews. Direct your requests to the publisher at the following addresses:

Reformation Heritage Books
2965 Leonard St. NE
Grand Rapids, MI 49525
616-977-0889
orders@heritagebooks.org
www.heritagebooks.org

Printed in the United States of America
21 22 23 24 25 26/10 9 8 7 6 5 4 3 2

ISBN 978-1-60178-564-0

For additional Reformed literature, request a free book list from Reformation Heritage Books at the above regular or e-mail address.

To

**Drs. Dennis Riff, Gilbert Roys, Joel Lester,
Timothy Nicholls,** and **Charles Hargon,**
as well as countless other medical specialists
who assisted in my fight for survival:
men and women of a noble profession
and valued skill.

*This is especially dedicated to all those who
are fighting for their lives against cancer.*

In the words of Sir Winston Churchill:
"Never, never, never give up."

HOW CAN I
HONOR CHRIST IN
FIGHTING CANCER?

Cancer is the most dreaded C word in the English language. It stuns and shocks people. When they are told they have cancer, most people find that their brains immediately become numb. Then, their minds burst suddenly with diverse uncontrollable thoughts and fears. Their imaginations run wild, and they conceive every kind of dark scenario. Cancer is a terrorizing disease!

According to the American Cancer Society, 1,658,370 people were diagnosed with cancer in 2015. Of those diagnosed, 36 percent died, or 589,430. At that time, it was predicted that another 30 to 35 percent of those diagnosed in 2015 would die in 2016. This is in spite of modern medical advancements. Also, according to the American Cancer Society, "39.6% of all men and women will be diagnosed with cancer at some point in their lifetime." This means that four out of every ten people reading this will be diagnosed with cancer in the future.

2   How Can I Honor Christ in Fighting Cancer?

Almost everyone diagnosed with cancer will endeavor to fight it; a few simply give up and refuse medical treatment. As a cancer survivor, I encourage everyone diagnosed with cancer to fight it. Yes, seek medical treatment and use every earthly means possible to fight cancer. The fight I am primarily interested in, however, is not medical but spiritual. This spiritual fight, conducted in a manner that honors Christ the Creator and Lord, will aid your medical fight tremendously. Through my experience and a series of practical lessons derived from it and from Scripture, you can better understand what this kind of fight looks like.

HOW IT BEGAN FOR ME

It was an unforgettable morning: Pearl Harbor Day, December 7, 2004. My wife Debby was driving me to the hospital for a colonoscopy. For nine months I had been fighting fatigue and had grown weaker and weaker. My appetite virtually disappeared, and two or three bites of even my favorite meals would fill me. Soon, I started losing all taste for food. Waiting in the car while Debby was grocery shopping (I felt too weak to help), I thought to myself, *I have nothing to live for.* Slowly, I came to realize that I was actually depressed. Those who know me can verify that this is contrary to my personality. I knew I needed to see a doctor.

A primary care physician determined from my blood work that I was anemic and hypoglycemic. He

How It Began for Me 3

assured me these problems could be easily cured with over-the-counter iron tablets and exercising. I started taking the iron and working out several times a week but kept getting weaker and was easily fatigued.

Knowing that something was desperately wrong, I made an appointment with a gastroenterologist, who scheduled me for a colonoscopy. When I awakened from the colonoscopy, the nurse rushed me into the doctor's office. He told me that I had stage 3 colon cancer. Pearl Harbor Day took on new meaning for me. Two days later, on December 9, I had surgery to remove the cancer, and the surgeon removed 20 percent of my colon. One week later, due to a post-op bacterial infection, or sepsis, that had invaded my abdominal and chest cavities, doctors operated again to prepare me for my third surgery. I was diagnosed with adult respiratory distress syndrome (ARDS), a serious disease that attacked the lining of my lungs as a result of the sepsis. During the third surgery, my lungs collapsed, my kidneys shut down, and my heart stopped. The surgeon revived me, removed another 15 percent of my colon, and sought to destroy the infection. Two days later, infectious disease and kidney specialists joined to assist in combating the infection. (For ten days I was connected to a ventilator, and tubes were in my mouth, nose, three sections of my abdomen, and my neck.) On Saturday, after the third surgery, I briefly opened and closed my eyes to see six doctors standing around my bed in the ICU. These doctors apprised my wife that they

4   How Can I Honor Christ in Fighting Cancer?

had done all they could do, and they did not think I would make it through the night. They said that it was now up to me. An elder in our church reported to me later that my wife told the doctors, "No, sirs, it is not up to him, but to the Lord Christ in heaven."

During the third surgery, I felt I was dying. Contrary to the way death is portrayed today, it is not a bright, shining light at the end of a tunnel, warm and inviting. Rather, it was dark, cold, and frightening. I sensed I was being jostled around on the operating table, not knowing that doctors were fighting to keep me alive. Even under anesthesia, I felt pain scream through my body. As the reality of death gripped my soul, the Spirit of God brought glorious comfort to my mind: "Yea, though I walk through the valley of the shadow of death, I will fear no evil; for thou art with me; thy rod and thy staff they comfort me" (Ps. 23:4). I kept repeating this verse in my mind. You see, the psalmist had a principled determination encountering death. Regardless of how horrible and ugly death appeared, he purposed he would fear *no* evil. Why? He knew the Lord was with him and that with His rod He would either drive away death, or with His staff he would lead the psalmist through the shadowed valley to the other side. Whichever it would be, Christ the Lord was the Shepherd of his life *and* death, and he would be safe.

Later, my wife and church secretary were informed that churches, pastors, and friends — literally from all around the world — had special prayer

How It Began for Me 5

for me either that Saturday night or the next Lord's Day. God was pleased to hear their prayers, and the next day, the Lord's Day, shortly after noon my wife awakened me with tears of joy. She said my kidneys had started functioning and everything appeared to be returning to normal. Seven days later the tubes and the ventilator were removed. On December 31, my chief surgeon released me from the hospital. What was supposed to have been a five-to-six-day hospital stay ended up being twenty-three days. Three weeks later, January 19, 2005, though extremely weak, I began a series of chemotherapy treatments that ended on June 22, 2005.

My oncologist told me that when I finished the chemo treatments, I should have forty-plus years to live. I assured him that whether I lived another four days or forty years, my great comfort was that He who ordained the days of my first and second births had also appointed the day and hour of my death. Nothing can alter that. I rejoice now that every day is a good day, and I have purposed that with every fiber of my being I will endeavor to live to the glory of Christ my God and be a blessing to as many people as possible. It is good to be alive! Though I would not wish what I experienced upon the worst criminal in the world, I would not exchange it for anything. God's peace that flooded my soul from the moment of diagnosis until now, Christ's presence that I sensed so near, and the Holy Spirit's sovereign grace that bolstered me during many painful days

6   How Can I Honor Christ in Fighting Cancer?

have been worth it all. How precious are God's gracious gifts, many of which can only be experienced in suffering and affliction. As the psalmist says, "It is good for me that I have been afflicted" (119:71).

HOW DO YOU GO FORWARD AND FIGHT?

If you are reading this, I assume you or someone you know and love has been diagnosed with cancer. You want help or desire to help someone. I am not a medical professional. If you have medical questions, ask qualified doctors. I write this as a Christian, an ordained minister of the gospel, and a cancer survivor of thirteen years. The lessons I share here are deeply personal insights borne out of my own suffering and struggles and efforts to help others. From the moment of diagnosis, I prayed that I would honor Christ, that I would not say or do anything to discredit His magnificent name, and that I would help others see the reality of the power of the gospel in my life. That is still my goal and the goal of this booklet. The series of lessons that follow can guide you through dark and difficult times. They brought me much comfort and strength, and I pray they will likewise help you.

ACKNOWLEDGE THAT YOUR CANCER IS
IN GOD'S PROVIDENCE

When a person is diagnosed with cancer, questions begin to emerge immediately: Why me? Why now? What is going to happen? What have I done

Acknowledge that Cancer Is in God's Providence 7

wrong? Fear settles in, and nightmarish thoughts invade your mind, accompanied by more questions: Will there be surgery? Will I have chemo, and will it make me too sick to go to work? Women especially have questions about their natural glory: Will I lose my hair? Other questions bombard the mind quicker than you can reason through them. Who will provide for my spouse and care for my children if I die? Should I be making out a will? Then you begin to identify with Job, the ancient patriarch: "For the thing which I greatly feared is come upon me, and that which I was afraid of is come unto me" (Job 3:25). The dreaded C word has come to your house.

There is a comforting answer to all these questions. It is called the providence of God. You may wonder, what is God's providence? The best biblical definition I know is the Westminster Shorter Catechism, question 11, "What are God's works of providence?" The answer: "God's works of providence are His most holy (Psalm 145:17), wise (Psalm 104:24; Isaiah 28:29), and powerful preserving (Hebrews 1:3) and governing all His creatures, and all their actions (Psalm 103:19; Matthew 10:29, 31)."

Understand what wise Solomon wrote: "To every thing there is a season, and a time to every purpose under the heaven:… a time to weep, and a time to laugh; a time to mourn, and a time to dance" (Eccl. 3:1, 4). You have laughed and enjoyed life, and now it is time to weep and mourn. Furthermore, what you should understand is that this cancer—yes, this

8 How Can I Honor Christ in Fighting Cancer?

horrible cancer—is from the Lord. If you attribute it to blind chance or luck, or worse, to fate that is arbitrary and cruel, you have no lasting comfort. If things randomly happen throughout the universe without order or reason and you imagine that everybody has bad luck or bad karma sometime or other, you are robbed of any peace. Blaming the devil is even worse. Believing that Satan sneaked past the eyes of almighty God and hit you with cancer or that God didn't see it coming or was powerless to stop it will only open you up to more mental anguish—what will the devil do next?

God the Lord revealed a truth to His ancient prophet Isaiah that should settle all plaguing questions and bring stability to your soul: God desires that His people "may know from the rising of the sun, and from the west, that there is none beside me. I am the Lord, and there is none else; I form the light, and create darkness: I make peace, and create evil: I the Lord do all these things" (Isa. 45:6–7; cf. Amos 3:6). Notice the diversity of what God does: He forms light and creates darkness; He makes peace and creates calamity. Observe the extent of what the Almighty does: *all these things.* This conforms to what the apostle Paul declares in the New Testament: "In [Him] also we have obtained an inheritance, being predestinated according to the purpose of him who worketh all things after the counsel of his own will" (Eph. 1:11). This means that God is working out His foreordained

Interact with a Sharper Healing Instrument   **9**

purpose in your life—this very moment—through the ordinary circumstances of His providence.

God, who is all powerful, easily could have kept you perfectly healthy until your dying day. He could have stopped the cancer from developing and attacking your vital organs, but He did not. He brought cancer into your life for a purpose and allowed it at this exact moment. Acknowledge that this dreaded disease, which could kill you in the future, is from the wise, kind, and benevolent hand of God's providence. Samuel Medley, an old hymn writer, grasped this divine truth when he penned these words: God is "too wise to be mistaken, He, too good to be unkind." This is the first lesson in honoring Christ as you fight cancer.

INTERACT WITH A HEALING INSTRUMENT SHARPER THAN A SURGEON'S SCALPEL

If you have not yet had surgery, you may go into the operating room soon. If you have had surgery, the surgeon skillfully entered your body and excised the deadly cancer (or as much of it as possible) with a scalpel. The scalpel was sharper than any known razor; otherwise, it could not have done its necessary work without causing further damage. Though often viewed as a scary device, it is a healing instrument. It seems that there is nothing sharper than the surgeon's scalpel.

Actually, though, there is something sharper. It cannot cut the body, but it can pierce and penetrate

10   How Can I Honor Christ in Fighting Cancer?

the soul, the spirit, and the mind. It can read your thoughts. What is this instrument for healing? It is the Holy Bible, which Paul calls "the sword of the Spirit" (Eph. 6:17). The writer of Hebrews describes it this way: "The Word of God is quick, and powerful, and sharper than any twoedged sword, piercing even to the dividing asunder of soul and spirit, and of the joints and marrow, and is a discerner of the thoughts and intents of the heart" (4:12).

When you pick up the Holy Bible, you have in your hand the greatest book in the entire world. It is the Book of books and is known as the Scriptures. The Holy Bible is the very mind and word of God inerrantly given in written form to humankind. God, by the Holy Spirit, moved on its writers, who wrote down the very words of God. It is not a book of human beings, but the one and only book from God. The apostle Peter affirms, "Knowing this first, that no prophecy of the scripture is of any private interpretation. For the prophecy came not in old time by the will of man: but holy men of God spake as they were moved by the Holy Ghost" (2 Peter 1:20–21). Paul describes the Holy Bible in this manner: "All scripture is given by inspiration of God, and is profitable for doctrine, for reproof, for correction, for instruction in righteousness" (2 Tim. 3:16).

To describe the greatness of the Word of God, an unknown author penned the following:

The Holy Bible contains the mind of God, the state of man, the way of salvation, the doom of sinners, and the happiness of believers. Its doctrines are holy, its precepts are binding, its histories are true, and its decisions are immutable. Read it to be wise, believe it to be safe, and practice it to be holy. It contains light to direct you, food to support you, and comfort to cheer you. It is the traveler's map, the pilgrim's staff, the pilot's compass, the soldier's sword, heaven opened, and the gates of hell disclosed. Christ is its grand object, our good its design, and the glory of God its end. It should fill the memory, rule the heart, and guide the feet. Read it slowly, frequently, and prayerfully. It is a mine of wealth, a paradise of glory, and a river of pleasure. It is given you in life, shall be opened in judgment, and will be remembered forever. It involves the highest responsibilities, will reward the greatest labor, and will condemn all who trifle with its sacred contents.

When I was diagnosed with cancer, my doctor gave me resources to digest; my surgeon gave me more. In the hospital, a chaplain, desiring to impart peace and inspire hope, gave me motivational materials to read. They all served their purpose, but nothing could compare with the living and written Word of God. During my hospital stay and my first two weeks at home, I was so weak that I could not hold a glass, much less my Bible. My dear wife read to me from the Scriptures at least three times a day. Words cannot describe the comfort, peace, joy, strength, assurance, and grace that flowed through my mind and soul as I heard and applied God's Word.

During my hospital stay, the TV was on constantly, usually turned to a news channel. I asked the nurses to turn it off, but they would not, because, they said, I needed something to occupy my mind. During the months I underwent chemo, I visited a fellow sufferer in his home who was dying from mesothelioma. At every visit I found him glued to the TV, sad and blue. It is easy for cancer patients to fall into this complacent posture, because TV does occupy the mind—but not with the eternal things that matter most. The sharpest instrument for healing is the Holy Bible. Read it daily or have someone read it to you; interact with it in every way possible. In this way you honor Christ as you fight cancer.

FIND MEANING AND FULFILLMENT IN LIFE IN HIM WHO IS THE RESURRECTION AND THE LIFE

In his *Confessions*, the early church father Augustine wrote these words: "Man, this small portion of creation, wants to praise You. You stimulate him to take pleasure in praising You, because You have made us for Yourself, and our hearts are restless until they find their rest in You." People are restless. Easily bored, they go from one new "toy" to another, from one new fad or fashion to the next, from one new place or church to the next alternative. Like the waves of a

Find Meaning and Fulfillment in Life 13

storm-tossed sea, they go back and forth, without any sense of direction, meaning, and fulfillment in life.

Cancer patients, especially if they do not know Christ as Lord and Savior, are often the same. They seek to escape their pain and fear. They try to drown out the voice of a screaming conscience with different things. When one effort does not work, they try something else. They seek to find comfort from friends who tell them they are okay and are going to a better place, when in reality their minds tell them otherwise. They become restless. For those who are restless, there is a word of invitation. Jesus says, "Come unto me, all ye that labour and are heavy laden, and I will give you rest" (Matt. 11:28). There is no bodily, mental, emotional, or spiritual rest like that found in Christ the Lord. Find rest in Him today!

Too often, cancer patients lose any sense of meaning in life. Fearing that their life is nearly over, many give up. Some cancer patients utter hopeless statements: "There is no meaning in life for me now. My dreams are shattered. My hopes are stolen. All that I planned to accomplish has disappeared. My life is empty." That is a self-defeating attitude. Even if your doctors have said that you have six months, a year, or maybe two to live, your life still has meaning, and you can find fulfillment in the present. Life's meaning and fulfillment are not found in who you are or what you do, but in a person—Jesus the Christ, the resurrection and the life.

14   How Can I Honor Christ in Fighting Cancer?

As Jesus stood outside a desert tomb of a friend, the dead man's sister lamented that Jesus was not there before her brother died. In the midst of this sadness, Jesus spoke these immortal, hope-filled words: "I am the resurrection, and the life: he that believeth in me, though he were dead, yet he shall live. And whoever liveth and believeth in me shall never die. Believest thou this?" (John 11:25–26). The apostle Paul, under the sentence of death and awaiting execution, echoed that faith and exclaimed, "According to my earnest expectation and my hope, that in nothing I shall be ashamed, but with all boldness, as always, so now also Christ shall be magnified in my body, whether it be by life, or by death. For to me, to live is Christ, and to die is gain" (Phil. 1:20–21). Paul desired that in his body, whether by life or death, Christ would be magnified. This brought meaning and a profound sense of fulfillment to him, even under the sentence of death. Death, for the apostle, was not a senseless loss but a great and eternal gain. The same can be true for you as well.

Your earthly life is not over until it is over. You may have months and even years to live. Until you draw your final breath and your earthly life is ended, glorify God, worship His Son, gather with His church, immerse yourself in His word, resist fears and doubts, and reach out to others with Jesus's life-giving message of living water and the bread of life. Finding meaning and fulfillment in life in the One who is the resurrection and the life is an important lesson in honoring Christ as you fight cancer.

REFUSE TO GIVE IN TO FEAR—FIGHT IT

One young lady recently diagnosed with cancer for the second time said to me, "I'm afraid, Pastor."

I replied, "Of course you are; it's only natural. We're not playing tiddlywinks; we're dealing with issues of life and death."

Fear is a real entity, an essence that actually exists. Some cancer patients give an outward appearance that everything is fine, but inwardly an unhealthy fear is consuming them. They attempt to keep a stiff upper lip and smile when they are around others. Casual observers think the person is handling cancer well. Meanwhile, when no one is around, their minds are assaulted with doubts, emotional anguish, and untamed fears that molest the soul. In bed at night, many cancer patients shed silent tears that are birthed by an unhealthy fear of the unknown. That is why the psalmist wrote about being "afraid for the terror by night" and "the pestilence that walketh in darkness" (Ps. 91:5–6).

Yet there is a healthy fear that is wholesome. It is the fear of the Lord, which is the beginning of all true knowledge and wisdom (see Prov. 1:7; 9:10). An old writer once stated, "The person that fears the Lord need not fear." How true! There is an unhealthy fear, however, that is poisonous. It must be resisted. Allow me to illustrate.

16 How Can I Honor Christ in Fighting Cancer?

I will never forget my first day of chemotherapy treatment. Though treatment centers vary in different geographical locations, the Los Angeles hospital where I was treated had a special chemo room. It was rectangular, with eighteen posh reclining chairs arranged along the walls. The recliners held blankets and pillows for the patients to use during treatments; the various chemos are kept in cold storage until injected into the patients. Treatments can take up to five hours to complete; hence, the recliners and pillows help to relax patients, and the blankets keep them warm. When I walked in and looked at the patients with IVs in their arms or ports through which flowed chemicals of assorted colors, one element filled the atmosphere of the room—fear. Among the patients there was little talking and no smiles, and fright was written all over their faces. It was heaviness, a fear that could be felt, and it almost overwhelmed me.

I realized that I was at a crossroad. I could yield to the gloomy fear that pervaded the room, or I could fight it. Which would be worse—yielding to the depressing gloom and joining the misery or fighting it with all my ransomed powers? Either way, I knew the next five months would be indescribably tough. Again, the Holy Scriptures brought me direction and determination: "Yea, though I walk through the valley of the shadow of death, *I will fear no evil*: for thou art with me; thy rod and thy staff they comfort me" (Ps. 23:4, emphasis added). Immediately, the way ahead was clear. Like the psalmist David, with a principled determination, I purposed not to fear the evil disease that was threatening my life or to yield to the terror it brought.

With fear comes bondage. Fear brings you into bondage to itself in several ways: by weakening and impeding the body's natural healing processes, by depressing the spirit, and by tormenting the mind and soul. If you fear something, irrational and morbid thoughts bounce around your mind like ping-pong balls. When fear is in control, it does a lot of damage. John, the beloved apostle, understood this when he wrote, "There is no fear in love; but perfect love casteth out fear: because fear hath torment. He that feareth is not made perfect in love. We love him, because he first loved us" (1 John 4:18–19). Did you catch the apostle's words "fear hath torment"? The great love that God has for His people, and their subsequent love to Him, casts out assaulting fear and torment and brings wonderful peace. That is why the apostle Paul, while in a dark prison awaiting death, wrote to the young pastor Timothy: "For God hath not given us the spirit of fear; but of power, and of love, and of a sound mind" (2 Tim. 1:7).

MAINTAIN A SENSE OF HUMOR

"Maintain a sense of humor?" you might ask. "Are you kidding me? Have a sense of humor in the midst of my terrible pain and in the face of possible death? This is not a laughing matter." Yes, that is exactly

18   How Can I Honor Christ in Fighting Cancer?

what I am saying. And you are correct: cancer is not a laughing matter. But you can either sit around depressed, feeling sorry for yourself, or you can enjoy the life God is presently giving you and find a healing humor in selected things. I believe this is what Solomon meant when he wrote these words: "A merry heart doeth good like a medicine: but a broken spirit drieth the bones" (Prov. 17:22). Let me share an anecdote.

Two months into chemo treatments, my oncologist sent me to my gastroenterologist for a check-up. Providentially, I met him in the hallway leading to his office. He is about 6 feet 6 inches tall and is from Brooklyn, New York. When he saw me, he hugged me, stood back, put both hands on my shoulders, and in a sympathetic tone said, "I've heard that you've been through a really rough time. How much of your colon did Dr. Roys remove?"

I replied, "The first surgery he removed 20 percent, and the third surgery he removed an additional 15 percent." Then I added, "I no longer have a colon."

He gave me a puzzled look and firmly said, "Yes you do!"

And I said, "No sir, I don't."

Then with a stern look, speaking in his heavy Brooklyn accent, he asserted, "Yes you do; you have sixty-five percent left. I'm your doctor; I know!"

To which I replied, "No sir, I don't. Most people have a colon, and I once had one, but now I have a semicolon. If it gets down to a comma, I'm gonna get nervous, and if it gets down to a period, I'm really gonna start sweatin' bullets."

He erupted into a barrel-chested laugh that could be heard (I thought) throughout the hospital. Still laughing, he hugged me again and said, "That's hilarious. I'm going to use that with my patients. Most of them need cheering up."

There is no escaping the indescribable pains, aches, throbs, radiation burns, sores, chemo nausea, vomiting, and diarrhea that come with fighting cancer. But we can occasionally inject a dose of "a time to laugh" to help lighten the load. Certain things can be genuinely humorous; honor Christ your Creator and make good use of them.

REALIZE THAT EVERY DAY IS A GOOD DAY, A GIFT FROM GOD

When you are fighting cancer, days can be long and drawn out; the nights, even worse. Some days you feel a little better and a ray of hope shines in. Unexpectedly, the next day is just the opposite. Every joint and muscle, from the top of your head to the soles of your feet, throbs with pain. The prescribed pain medication helps but does not take it away. If you can walk, you are often weak and slow, and it is difficult to move around. (I remember when I started walking with a cane; it would often take five minutes for me to walk from the sofa in our family room to our bedroom.) You are sore in places you never dreamed. Often, you are in a foul mood and nothing magically appears to remedy it. Even the days when the sun shines the brightest don't seem to help. You look at everything through dark-colored glasses, and nothing is coming up roses. A few bad days can be tolerated, but when day after day brings the same unrelenting agony and persistent hurting, depression sneaks in and becomes your constant companion. Is there any relief?

Relief can be found in viewing every day in one of two ways. Understand that thinking wrongly can make you feel worse, and thinking correctly can help you feel better. That is why Paul wrote, "Be ye transformed by the renewing of your mind" (Rom. 12:2). The first way to view each day is to realize that it is a good day. "Really?" you might ask. "Do you know how sick I feel? The smell of food makes me nauseous, and when I try to eat, nothing stays down. Don't you know that I can't even go to the bathroom by myself?" I know; I've been there and done that. Nevertheless, the words of the psalmist are true: "Blessed be the Lord, who daily loadeth us with benefits, even the God of our salvation" (68:19). This truth causes days to look differently. God loads you daily with benefits! You are alive. You have another day to enjoy God's good earth and its beauty. You have family and friends (hopefully) who love and tenderly care for you. (If you don't have anyone in your life and you are in the hospital or in a hospice, ask a caregiver to phone a pastor. Ask the pastor to come and visit you. If that pastor is a true man of God and he pastors a healthy church, from that moment you will have someone in your life who loves and cares for you. That is the great blessing of the covenant community, which is called the church.) There are many blessings and benefits that make each day a good one, if you will start looking for them.

The second way to view each day is to know that it is a gift from God. Holy Scripture teaches that in God "we live, and move, and have our being" (Acts 17:28). Also, "every good gift and every perfect gift is from above, and cometh down from the Father of lights, with whom is no variableness, neither shadow of turning" (James 1:17). Yes, even today is a gift of God. His mercies and compassions are new upon you every morning, even this morning. That is what the prophet Jeremiah meant when he looked over the ruined and desolate city of Jerusalem and wrote, "It is of the LORD's mercies that we are not consumed, because His compassions fail not. They are new every morning: great is thy faithfulness. The LORD *is* my portion, saith my soul; therefore will I hope in him" (Lam. 3:22–24). Though everything looked bleak and dismal, Jeremiah knew that God's covenant mercies and compassions were new upon him that morning. And though you are hurting and possibly depressed, recognize that God has this morning shown you great mercy and compassion. Realizing that every day is a good day and that

22 How Can I Honor Christ in Fighting Cancer?

it is a gift from God's throne is yet another lesson in honoring Christ as you fight cancer.

SEEK TO HELP, ENCOURAGE, AND BLESS SOMEONE EACH DAY

It is easy to become self-absorbed when you are battling cancer. After all, it is your life that is at stake. There are scheduled times to take medications, regular appointments for radiation or chemo treatments, the hours it takes to travel to treatment centers and for the treatments themselves, frequent trips to one or more doctors, colostomies or catheter bags to empty and clean, creams to apply for radiation burns, physical therapy sessions to help regain strength, and the list could go on. Along with the pain and recovery efforts, there are lingering doubts about the operation's success and nagging questions about the treatments: Did the surgeons get all the cancer? Will the treatments be successful? Will I go into remission? How much longer do I have to live? These activities and uncertainties are time-consuming and energy-draining. Furthermore, they naturally cause us to focus on ourselves. So often, we forget about others. We forget that there are others who are worse off than we are. It is easy to forget that there are cancer patients with little or no hope. They may be single, widowed, divorced, or, for whatever reason, they may be a long way from home, family, and friends. They may return to an empty house or apartment, and there is no one who really cares for them.

Seek to Help, Encourage, and Bless Someone 23

Again, we find direction in God's Word. Christ's kingdom is opposite to the kingdoms of this world. In His kingdom, the way up is down; the way to be first is to be last; the way to increase is to decrease; the way to be exalted is to be humble; and the way to receive is to give. Jesus taught that it is more blessed to give than to receive (Acts 20:35). It sounds strange, doesn't it? Yet this is the manner God our Creator and Redeemer ordained that His kingdom should advance. Consider this proverb: "The liberal soul shall be made fat: and he that watereth shall be watered also himself" (11:25). Every time I water my wife's beautiful plants, as I roll up the garden hose I notice water has splashed on me. That is the teaching of this proverb. When we spiritually water others, blessings splash back on us.

On the first day of chemo treatments, after I overcame the initial shock of the overwhelming fear filling the room, I purposed to introduce myself to every patient and resolved to encourage and bless them. I kindly greeted them and asked how they were, gave them gospel literature to read, told them I was praying for them (which I did), and sought to encourage each in his or her particular need. It helped me to remember the model set by Jesus, the Lord of glory who came down from heaven as the Son of man: "The Son of man came not to be ministered unto, but to minister, and to give his life a ransom for many" (Matt. 20:28). Jesus also said, "For whether is greater, he that sitteth at meat, or he

24   How Can I Honor Christ in Fighting Cancer?

that serveth? is not he that sitteth at meat? but I am among you as he that serveth" (Luke 22:27). Jesus, the One who should have been ministered to and served, came to serve God the Father and minister to others. What a model!

Instead of being glued to a TV or sitting in a dark room feeling sorry for yourself, start thinking about who could use some encouragement and blessing. Make a list of people and start praying for them. Then think of ways you can enrich their lives in their battles with cancer or whatever struggle they are enduring. If you are physically able, go visit and take them a milkshake. Always read some Scripture and pray with them before leaving. Be genuinely concerned about their lives and well-being. If you are not physically able to visit, give someone a phone call, write a note, or send a card. Always include a suggested portion of Scripture to read and let them know that you are praying for them. You will find your soul enriched with blessing.

BELIEVE THAT EVEN THIS CANCER IS FOR YOUR GOOD

One day a forty-one-year-old cancer patient said, "Why has this happened to me? My career was just taking off, I am almost out of debt, my children are ready to graduate from high school and head off to college, and everything was sailing along beautifully. Now I'm on disability, my wife has had to go to work, and we're just barely keeping ahead of

Believe that Even this Cancer Is for Your Good 25

our creditors. Why has this nightmare happened to me now?" His doctors had just told him that he has perhaps two to three years to live, and his questions reflect the sentiments of many cancer patients.

Thankfully, due to early detection and the advancements of modern medicine, some cancer patients are brought into a state of remission and are able, after extended periods of treatment, to resume work and a normal life. Others are not so blessed. Their cancers are terminal, and doctors have confirmed there is nothing more that can be done. Some are in the prime of life and some are elderly, while others are quite young. I took chemo with a healthy-looking young man in his late twenties who had played college football at USC. Careers are interrupted; some patients have poor insurance and are saddled with huge medical expenses; young mothers weep over their small children; and teenagers sadly wish they could have gotten married and had a family. All cancer patients, to one degree or another, view the disease as bad. And they are correct.

Yet there is another way of looking at your cancer: see it as good. "What?" you may shout. "How can something so terrible be good?" The answer is found in one of the most instructive and insightful passages in God's Word, Romans 8:28, which states, "And we know that all things work together for good to them that love God, to them who are the called according to his purpose." If you "love God" and are "the called according to His purpose," yes,

26 How Can I Honor Christ in Fighting Cancer?

cancer is good, because it is working for your ultimate spiritual good. "I don't understand," you may say. I understand your confusion, so allow me to unfold this verse and explain why your cancer can be viewed as good—good as God defines it, not as humans understand it.

Paul starts the verse with a positive outlook. There is no doubt, no second-guessing, no equivocation—but absolute certainty and assurance: "And we know." He then moves on to particulars: "all things." He does not say some, many, or most, but *all* things. This includes evil and bad entities, even your cancer. He proceeds to declare the divine pattern, that all the things you encounter in life "work together." While all things are not good in a relative sense (e.g., lying, divorce, theft, and murder), in God's great economy and plan He causes them all to work together in an absolute sense. Nothing is removed from His sovereign control. Everything is under His government and rule. Then Paul concludes that God's great and grand purpose in these collaborative workings is "for good." Indeed, because God is omnipotent and all-wise, He is able to weave the varying circumstances of your life into a pattern that brings about moral excellence and eternal good. This includes your cancer.

You may be thinking, "I understand generally what you're saying, but how is cancer good for me?" Perhaps it has caused you to slow down and quit living life in the fast lane. Perhaps it has caused you to abandon useless and frivolous idols of your heart.

Perhaps it has caused you to realign your priorities and embrace the issues that truly count. Perhaps it has caused you to turn toward more worthwhile pursuits. Perhaps it has caused you to value family and friends and spend more time with them. Most importantly, perhaps it has caused you to seek the spiritual subjects of eternity: God, His Son and the Savior Jesus Christ, His Word, His salvation, His church, holiness of life, and heaven. Only you can earnestly answer these questions. Whatever your station in life, if you believe that even this deadly disease is for your good, you honor Christ as you fight cancer.

DETERMINE THAT WHILE ONE DAY CANCER MAY KILL YOU, IT WILL NOT DEFEAT YOU

When I finished chemotherapy, my oncologist said that I was now considered "cancer prone." "Which means," he said, "that unless a freight train falls out of the sky and lands on you in your backyard, cancer will one day kill you. It's not a matter of *if* the cancer returns, but *when.*" *Oh great*, I thought, *now cancer is stalking me.* That gave me a sobering perspective on life, as it should all cancer patients. How then should we live in light of this grim reality?

One of the most soul-fortifying and comforting passages in God's Word is Romans 8:35–39:

> Who shall separate us from the love of Christ? shall tribulation, or distress, or persecution, or famine, or nakedness, or peril, or sword? As it is written, For thy sake we are killed all the

day long; we are accounted as sheep for the slaughter. Nay, in all these things we are more than conquerors through him that loved us. For I am persuaded, that neither death, nor life, nor angels, nor principalities, nor powers, nor things present, nor things to come, nor height, nor depth, nor any other creature, shall be able to separate us from the love of God, which is in Christ Jesus our Lord.

In verse 35, Paul lists seven realities that can possibly plague us: tribulation, distress, persecution, famine, nakedness, peril, and sword. These are extreme circumstances that can happen abruptly. He then lists in verses 38–39 the things human beings fear the most, and the first on the list is death. Our Creator has placed within everyone the instinctive desire to live and survive. We do everything possible to avoid death. That is why suicide, or self-murder, is so unnatural. Yet no matter how hard we try, death is ultimately unavoidable. Unless Christ returns in our lifetime, each of us will die. For cancer patients, this reality seems more imminent than for the average healthy person. The thought of death hangs over our heads like the proverbial sword of Damocles. It is never far from the forefronts of our minds. Almost every time we feel a sudden pain, the thought flashes into our mind, *Has the cancer come back*? *Is this finally it*? Once again, some feel panic and fear.

How can we handle these intrusive and molesting thoughts? The answer lies in verse 37, between

Determine that Cancer May Kill but Won't Defeat 29

the extremities of life and the things most feared. In this verse, Paul makes an astonishing and phenomenal pronouncement. It begins with the words, "Nay, in all these things." What things? The things listed before and after verse 37. Paul continues, "We are more than conquerors through him that loved us." Note carefully that we are not *just* conquerors. Observe the superlative: we are *more than* conquerors, which means superabounding conquerors. We conquer exceedingly! Furthermore, this conquering ability is *not* within us. Many self-help specialists will tell you otherwise: "You can do it. It's just mind over matter. Think positively and you can beat cancer." It is similar to what the six doctors told my wife as I lay dying: "It's now up to him." While you definitely need a positive mental attitude in fighting cancer, the power to be a superabounding conqueror cannot be found within. It lies outside of us. It is found "through him that loved us." The "him" is none other than Jesus Christ the Lord.

If you are a Christian, someone who has been genuinely born again by the Holy Spirit, you know something of the great and incomprehensible love of God. As the beloved apostle John wrote, "Herein is love, not that we loved God, but that he loved us, and sent his Son to be the propitiation for our sins" (1 John 4:10). The cross, where the infinite wrath of the infinite God was poured out for a finite period of time on Christ the Son to pay the penalty of sin, is where genuine love is found. Plus, in that love is

30 How Can I Honor Christ in Fighting Cancer?

found the power to be a superabounding conqueror, even if death does overtake you. As you suffer, you identify somewhat with Christ's sufferings and enter into communion with Him. This leads to sanctification giving way to glorification, which is what Paul meant in Philippians 3:10–11: "That I may know him, and the power of his resurrection, and the fellowship of his sufferings, being made conformable unto his death; if by any means I might attain unto the resurrection of the dead."

Death is stalking everyone, even those without cancer. Reject a defeatist attitude and fight cancer until your last breath through Christ who conquered death. In this way, whether your life is long or short, you will not be defeated. Entering heaven and dwelling with "the spirits of just men made perfect" and "Jesus the mediator of the new covenant" is not defeat, but glorious victory (see Heb. 12:22–24). Determining that one day cancer may kill you but not defeat you honors Christ as you fight cancer.

CONCLUSION

If you are a follower of the Lord Jesus Christ, if you have been saved by grace alone through faith alone in Christ alone, this I promise you: Jesus *will* heal you! He may use doctors and modern medicine to heal you in this lifetime, or He may in answer to effectual, fervent prayer sovereignly cure you, or He may call you home to be forever healed in His holy and loving heavenly presence. Whatever His sovereign purpose,

Conclusion 31

He will heal you. Believe this as you fight cancer, and in so doing, you will be cheered on your journey. More importantly, you will honor Christ the Lord and Savior, the only Mediator between God and man.

The hymn "Guide Me, O Thou Great Jehovah" brought me much comfort and hope during bleak times of suffering. Written by the distinguished Welsh hymn writer William Williams, it was both my song and my prayer. May it be yours also.

> Guide me, O Thou great Jehovah,
> Pilgrim through this barren land;
> I am weak, but Thou art mighty;
> Hold me with Thy powerful hand;
> Bread of heaven, Bread of heaven,
> Feed me till I want no more,
> Feed me till I want no more.
>
> Open now the crystal fountain,
> Whence the healing stream doth flow;
> Let the fire and cloudy pillar
> Lead me all my journey through.
> Strong Deliverer, strong Deliverer,
> Be thou still my Strength and Shield,
> Be thou still my Strength and Shield.
>
> When I tread the verge of Jordan,
> Bid my anxious fears subside.
> Death of death, and hell's Destruction,
> Land me safe on Canaan's side.
> Songs of praises, songs of praises
> I will ever give to Thee,
> I will ever give to Thee.